Mastering the sales mindset

*An in-depth, yet simplified analysis of
sales in the hospitality department*

Konstantinos Chatzimitakos

Table of contents

1

Introduction

For a few months now I've been thinking of writing this book. If you ask me who this book is geared towards I would say professionals working in the **hospitality department** (waiters, sommeliers, receptionists, managers, hotel staff etc), **salesmen** (mostly for the first part of the book because the practical part is different due to the distance between the seller and the buyer), but also **non-professionals** who are interested to see another perspective or at least my approach and understanding on sales. As we move on from chapter to chapter, you will understand that there are more uses of the things we will analyze, not only on sales but other sectors of life in general.

What separates this book from others is that it's missing 400 pages from the average book on sales. We all see these huge books on sales having endless pages with strategies and what exact words to use in each case etc. I built my approach on sales myself and what I understood is that no matter how many books with unlimited strategies and scenarios you read, you will always come across a situation that was not written any-where. You see there are 2 separate things, the first one is strategies and the second one is the **mindset**. Strategies can apply to certain situations with specific variables, while the mindset makes you adapt to ANY situation using your versatile way of perception and thinking. There is an old saying ''Give some-one a fish and he has food for a day. Teach someone **how** to fish and he has food for the rest of his life''. If you think about it, a strategy is nothing more than someone else's conclusion that has worked before for him on a specific scenario. It's not bad to read sales strategies but only to see different perspec-tives and as food for thought instead of using them as absolute guidelines. The format of this book is single-read, someone can read it very easily but also go through multiple reads in a rela-tively short amount of time for a better understanding of the critical parts. Me being a person with a short attention span on reading, I thought this to be the most effective way to transmit this knowledge while not becoming boring or include odd in-formation. Therefore, this book is focused more on building the mindset rather than giving endless scenarios that have worked in the past, so yes, this is not just another sales book!

Talking from my personal experience, throughout my 7 years of working in Hotels and high-end restaurants, I understood fairly quickly that sales were playing a major role wherever I went. I remember my first job working as a trainee-waiter at a 5-star hotel, where the Restaurant Manager was...let's say not the best example of a manager in terms of behavior and how he treated the staff. At the time I had 1 day off per week and he continuously found a reason to call me to work on my day off. As you can imagine, I got exhausted after some time until one day I told him that, If I could sell more than 100 Euros worth of wine during dinner, he would let me take my day off without calling me for work. Let me mention here that it was an All-In-clusive hotel and the guests had as much house wine as they liked for free so, for someone to sell 100 euros worth of bottled wine to the guests was really something back then. He laughed at me and agreed. By the end of the night, I sold 8 bottles of wine worth around 180 euros altogether. Nobody could believe It and neither could I, but It was something in the excitement of the prize that got me extremely motivated to succeed. I got my day off that day but the most important thing I gained was the understanding that I could benefit from sales and raise my value on what I was doing, even though in this specific example I had to do it just to get what I was supposed to get anyway.

With a good understanding of sales, the right mindset, and the right application you can use sales to ask for a raise in your salary, get the promotion you were looking for, improve your confidence, motivate yourself for seeking deeper knowledge in what you want to sell and most importantly, my golden rule, *make your employers need you more than you need them!*

Everything you will read in this book is based on my personal experience, without the use of specified vocabulary or many technical terms, as easy as possible to understand for the average person. It's all the results of the things I had to improve, all the things I did wrong and fixed afterward, and the endless hours I spent thinking about how to evolve on what I was doing. I believe sales is not a talent and everyone can improve significantly the more they practice it. My goal is to write a book my previous self would be glad to read back when I started working, and I will be happy even if I manage to help a single person with it.

2

The Mindset

The most important thing, not only on sales but on many things in life, is your *mindset.* No matter how many different techniques you learn on how to sell something, or how to reply to a certain situation, at some point you will come across a scenario you never thought of how to deal with. That's where the mindset comes in. When you get it right, you don't have to think about which technique to use or which is the best approach to sell something, because it comes naturally! When we talk about the right mindset In this specific subject it basically means improving two things:

1.Your *knowledge* of what you are selling

2.Your *confidence*

In order to improve your confidence, you need to improve your knowledge of what you are selling so these two major factors are bound to each other.

Role of Confidence & Knowledge

Being confident for other things in life like your personality or the way you look is good, but you will lose all of it the moment you fail to answer the first question your client asks about the product you are trying to sell.

Basically what knowledge does is, it gives you confidence which leads to the **abundance mindset** on sales!

Knowing how good your product is, knowing exactly what you are selling, and having a deeper knowledge of it, puts you in an abundant state where you don't have to push someone to buy it and this is what makes a customer think that you are genuinely suggesting a product of good value. Besides, even if you don't sell it to the first 10 people, you know that there is a good chance the next 10 people will buy it! That means your confidence level doesn't drop. At the same time, it puts you out of the needy state of scarcity where you look desperate to sell something which is super repulsive for a customer. I started to notice this early but it took me a while to master it and find the right balance. A classic example for me was when I had to sell a specific bottle of rose wine from North Greece which was not on the wine list anymore so I had to promote it on my own. I was approaching people with too much excitement (which is good if you find the balance and don't overdo it) until I tried a different approach on a young couple. I described the wine in a few words as well as the reason it is not on the list explaining that it was the last bottle of this year's vintage and we had to remove it (which was true) and that it was the *last chance for someone to taste it in our restaurant.* The man seemed interested but he was a bit hesitant so he told me ''Thank you, but I think we will go with the house wine tonight''. I immediately smiled and said ''Okay sir, thank you very much''. As soon as I turned my back to leave he called me back saying ''Wait a minute, I think we will go with what you suggest''. This is the power of selling something in an **abundant state**! Subconsciously, you make your customer feel that they probably lost a very good chance to buy something of good value. This is the mindset you have to develop!

Selling with knowledge vs without

I have been in both. For instance, I was selling wine without any knowledge of wine except some basic information. I won't tell you that I didn't have success selling it even without deep knowledge because there are some other virtues which can help you sell something and we will analyze further on, but what I can guarantee you is that I was selling way much more from the moment I decided to study wine and get my wine courses done. Getting an easy sale or selling something that is not that expensive is as far as you will go without knowledge in 90% of the situations.

As you may have noticed already, people may ask questions either to learn more information about what they are buying or to test you and see if you truly know what you are selling. In both situations what they are really saying is: ''Convince me!''. In both scenarios, without knowledge, you will lose the sale even if your client wanted to buy in the first place because you just failed to answer his question and you came across as some-one who is trying to sell because you maybe take some kind of commission for it.

There are ways to avoid a question but you can't avoid every single question every time. I will give an example and I want you to imagine yourself being an observer to the following situation. Let's say you are at a family dinner in an average restaurant and your dad is looking at the wine list. The waiter approaches and tries to suggest a very nice, yet not-so- cheap Merlot from Bordeaux. Your dad thinks for a bit and says ''Okay it seems like a nice choice, has it been through oak maturation?'' The waiter loses the smile that he had before and he says he will ask his manager. After 3 minutes he comes back and says ''Yes sir, the wine has been through barrel maturation''. Dad: ''Has it been through new oak or not; because I want to know if it will be a good pairing for my stake''. The waiter leaves again and he comes back saying that he is not sure about that and they will have to search on the internet. At that moment think of your point of view at this table. What is the perception you have of this wine and this waiter? Is it that he wants to suggest something good that he doesn't know anything about; or is it that it costs a good amount of money, and possibly he will get credit for selling it? Your dad finally answers ''Never mind, we will have the house wine which I'm sure will be fine''. This is a typical example of a **lost sale** due to a lack of knowledge. Apart from the sale, there is a good chance this waiter made the restaurant lose a customer too by acting non-professional and having a lack of knowledge.

On the other hand, there will be more difficult situations than this where even if you've done your homework, you will need your confidence aimed up too. I remember one time I had a customer when I was working as a Head Sommelier in the UK, who was visiting the restaurant about 2 times per month. Every single time he studied the wine list for about 15-20 minutes and he tried to find something that he believed would be wrong. For example, the first time he ordered something from me, It was a wine from a rare wine-making area and he wanted to see if the vintage was correct. Unfortunately for me, It was vintage 2005 while in the wine list was written as 2004. I would be lying to you If I said it didn't break my confidence at that point because it was my responsibility to have all this sorted. The next day I searched every single wine from the list to double-check the vintages and guess what, apparently it was the only one that was wrong! But at least now I was sure that the next time he can't do the same thing. Now you may ask yourself ''Why would somebody do such a thing'' and I would tell you I don't know! What I know is that you have to be prepared for every situation and never let your confidence level drop when you are trying to sell something.

Building the vibe

There are some things that you have to consider before you even start selling something. Let's start with the way you look. Yes, your **appearance** does matter! Let's say you have 2 people selling the same product in the exact same way. The first one is a bit unshaved, seems like he hadn't had a haircut for a while and his suit is wrinkled. The second one is shaved, his suit looks very well ironed and he looks very sharp in general. From which one would you prefer to buy the product? My guess is the second one.

Next and very important would be **hygiene**. You want to always be clean and have a nice smell following you when you approach someone because you make a better impression and of course for other obvious reasons as well.

After the appearance part, we go to the psychological factors you need to consider such as *your **energy***. You always need to have positive energy surrounding you especially when you try to convince someone about buying something! Nobody wants to buy anything from a rude, grumpy, or aggressive person! Try to always wear a smile and make the people you come in contact with feel better just because of the energy that you're sharing with them! We all have bad days, but try to avoid letting negative energies surround you when you want to sell something or when coming in contact with people in general. You can try to think positive things or another one that works for me is I sometimes sing a song in my head and immediately change my mood!

Maybe by that time, you think to yourself if all these things are as important as I portray them to be. The answer is, yes they are! The thing I understood and want to share with you about sales is that ***all this preparation and work in all aspects of yourself result in a 3-5 minute conversation with a client, which will determine either if you close the sale or not!*** Sometimes you will realize that if you don't do most of this stuff you won't even get the chance to talk to a customer even for that small amount of time. Basically what we are trying to do is, we do our best for our client to be in a positive state of mind, feeling comfortable with us, to be willing to hear what we have to say. People are too quick to make conclusions and all you have is 3 to 5 minutes (probably even less if you are selling through the phone) to make all their doubts disappear so, everything from the way you look, to the way you talk, to the way you make them feel matters! We will get deeper into the practical part on the second part of the book.

Role of honesty

Improving your skills in sales doesn't mean that you're trying to sell a bad product making it look like a good one. I mean that technically you could, but this is not my approach on it and certainly something I don't encourage or recommend you to do. I can guarantee you that in the long run, you will always have better results by building a relationship of honesty between you and your clients as opposed to making a good sale one time but having an unsatisfied customer at the end of the day.

The reason I believe that you will always have better results being honest in the long run is called **trust**! Being honest with someone makes him trust you and when you build this connection between you and the client you *control the sale*! From this point on it's at least 50% easier to sell whatever you want to the specific person, because his guard is down, while always

16

keeping in your mind the person's budget range and the amount of money he is willing to spend (at this point you most likely have a pretty good idea of how much money is this person willing to pay every time). I've had people coming to where I was working and make me do the choices for them knowing that I won't let them unsatisfied. Another thing is that it's easier, safer, and more effective to slowly raise the budget a person is willing to spend every time using their trust, rather than raising it in an instant which will make him suspicious of you. In addition to that, your connection of trust made a person come back to your restaurant, hotel, or call you back for his next purchase on the stock market. You could sell him the most expensive bottle of wine the first time he came, have him pay let's say 500 euros, and never see him again cause you seemed like you're after his money. On the other hand, you sold him something much more affordable, based on his personal taste and he paid let's say 120 euros, but this person is now coming back every week for dinner, so in the long run, honesty, which leads to trust, wins over being greedy.

You can't sell ice to an Eskimo

This is probably one of the most important things I want to address as far as the mindset part. All sales come to the understanding of one principle: ***You can't sell anything to anybody***! And that's completely fine. Don't let your confidence level drop because you couldn't sell a very expensive product to a person who was not willing to pay that much in the first place. In that case, you should have tried to push for something more affordable and get the maximum value possible from the specific individual. On another example, there are some days where someone just woke up and wanted to eat a steak and glass of wine and nothing more. Now even if that person can technically pay for much more than this, if he woke up like this that day, no matter how hard you try, you won't change his mind. No, you can't sell him the expensive meal you thought you would, neither the premium wine flight for his courses, on that day. And that's completely fine! As a matter of fact, you may also make him unhappy by pushing too hard and that's something we don't want to happen. Remember the ***abundance mindset***. You will have so many more people to deal with and you can't let a single circumstance, a wrong decision, or a false conclusion that led to a lost sale break your confidence and your positive energy!

It's very romantic to think that a good salesperson can literally sell anything to anybody but unfortunately, this is not how it works. What I can tell you for sure, is that a good salesperson can *add* something to the buyer's purchase and get maximum value, only If he has made the correct thoughts and conclusions on what this person is willing to spend.

It's a very thin line about closing a sale and losing a sale and all it takes to lose it is to push your client a bit out of his limits and scare him in various ways. That's the reason I insist on having everything in the right place when you're going for the sale, starting from your **appearance**, to your **knowledge**, to **the way you think**, **the way you talk,** and **the energy you reflect**!

Be Versatile!

A very common technique for salespeople in the stock-market is the use of a *script*. Basically what happens is, they write down a very detailed script of the sale they want to make according to their approach. After that, what they do is they think of possible scenarios and try to demonstrate with each other an imaginary conversation with a client where the client has all sorts of different questions and each time they have to adjust to each one of them in order to close the sale.

The difference when you are trying to sell something via personal contact and not from a distance (ex. From the telephone) is, you have to organize the **script in your head** and be a bit more careful because the person sitting in front of you can not only notice the tone of your voice and what you say to him but other things as well.

Other than that, you just follow the same technique. You have a standard script in your mind for the specific individual and after that, you have to be *versatile*! You will double the chances of selling something when you counter your client's doubts as opposed to sticking with the same words every time without considering other factors in each different scenario. You have to be able to answer this person's questions, make him feel safe and secure to buy from you and this is where the right mindset kicks in.

The development on all the aspects of yourself we were talking about before, is leading to this exact moment where you now have 3 to 5 minutes to convince someone to buy your product. Knowledge of your product, a good appearance, positive energy, confidence will all have to be in the right place and you can't skip any of them. Will there be times where you will sell something even though you are not feeling the best version of yourself and you lack some of these things? Yes! But if you want to be consistent, you have to make the effort, maximize your sales and not just rely on luck or a random incident.

3

The approach

Now that we have mentioned the preparation for your personal development let's assume you feel the best version of yourself physically and psychologically and we will have a deeper look at the specific things for the moment of action. From now on I will analyze my personal procedure that I follow each time I want to sell something as well as some techniques and thoughts. After that, we will address some important things concerning the subject.

Selling procedure:

Evaluation of the customer

A sale starts the very first moment you see your customer. At this point, I will talk about my point of view so if you are working in a different place just keep the procedure rather than the specific questions I mention. You can adjust your own questions according to your situation the moment you understand how this works. The main thing I'd like you to gain from the whole procedure is the building of a script, which starts now.

What can you understand about your customer's financial situation? Is he wearing an expensive suit? Is he wearing a Rolex watch? Did you see him walk out of an expensive car or yacht? Maybe his lady is wearing an expensive designer bag? Do you have any information or special requests about the reservation he made? Did he ask for the best table in the restaurant? All these are signs you are dealing with a person in a very good financial situation and this is the first thing you start building your script with. On the other hand, If you can't notice any of these, start your script with this clue, that this person is not wearing anything fancy and seems like an average person. This is what you can understand from what you see and this is the first thing you will write down to your mind's notepad, to proceed and build your approach. Of course, the evaluation step is not to be prejudiced against anyone or show more attention to a rich person for example, but to build your script and know how to get the maximum value (we will talk about that further on), from each different individual.

Evaluation of the situation

The very next thing we want is to *evaluate the situation*. Having a clue on the person's financial situation is very helpful but you also have to consider the specific moment for your mind's script.

What information do you have for the specific day? Is it a special day for this person? Is it his daughter's birthday? Is it his anniversary with his wife? Is it a wedding? Is it his birthday? Is it just a regular lunch meal after work? Is it a business meeting with his colleagues? Is it a dinner date?

At this point, you may think to yourself: How can I know if it is any of these? Well, it's not that hard to understand but you need to practice and search for clues. For example, on a birthday it will be pretty obvious because, someone is going to wish a happy birthday to the specific person at some point, or the whole party will hold balloons or something. Maybe things are made easy for you by knowing it beforehand from the reservation (many people tend to make a notice on special occasions). If someone is on a date you have to observe his body language, for instance, does he seem a bit nervous or did he stand up for the lady to sit first or fix the chair for her? In the case of a business meeting, you may see many people with suits on, talking quite formally, etc.

Now, each situation has different limits to where you can push for a sale. If you have a clue on the financial situation of this person combined with the specific situation taking place that day you have 85% of the information you need to build your approach. The remaining 15% consists of other things that most of the times you don't know until you find out in person such as if this person drinks alcohol or not or if this person is vegan, or if there is a conflict going on at the table and nobody is really in the mood to spend extra money except the basic stuff.

Aiming for maximum value

The evaluation of the financial and the specific situation taking place leads to the next part in your script with would be reaching for the *maximum value* from the specific person.

Lower Limit   Maximum value   Overvalue

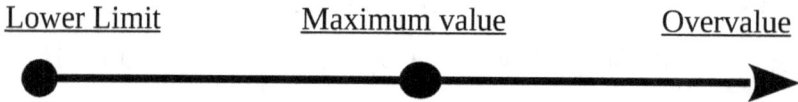

This is the shape that I always have in mind and it consists of different information and variables depending on the evaluation process. The lower limit is where you start, the maximum value is the point you want to reach and it's different for every individual based on the evaluation process. For instance, the *maximum value* for a person you evaluated high on both the financial and specific situation could be let's say 400 Euros for a good bottle of champagne and for a person you evaluated as average 30 Euros for a bottle of wine. All it matters to you is to get maximum value from both these people, thus moving the first dot, starting from the lower limit to go as close to the maximum value point as possible! Overvalue is the point where your customer was willing to pay less than you thought and you forced a sale with the danger of making him unhappy and losing trust in you.

There are three potential outcomes:

● 1. Your script and your approach were on point and you reached *maximum value*.

● 2. Your script was correct but your approach was not the best possible so you couldn't reach maximum value or, your script was not correct and even though you made a very good approach, this person was willing to pay much more than you thought. In both those cases, we are talking about *lost value*.

● 3. You made a very good approach but your script was incorrect and you managed to sell something that has the risk of leaving your customer unhappy because he paid so much for it the moment he was not willing to. In this case we are talking about *overvaluation*.

If you wonder how is it possible to sell something that the other person doesn't really want, I will explain it to you. If you develop this mindset and practice these techniques you will reach a point where you will be very good at selling something. You can become so good that you can even *manipulate* someone with how smoothly you make the approach to buy what you want to sell either by making him feel comfortable for a couple of moments with his decision (and probably regret it later) or by making him feel embarrassed in front of the table if he refuses to buy what you are selling in such a smooth way. Whatever the case may be I want to make this clear that *you should **always prefer to have a satisfied customer with the maximum value you can get from them rather than taking the risk to overvalue and have an unhappy, angry, or disappointed client at the end of the day.*** This is my point of view, what I think is more profitable in the long run but also morally correct!

Meaning of Specialization and finding the best product for each individual

Your knowledge of the product you want to sell plays a major role and gives you the **specialization** needed to find the best product for each individual.

For me, it was the knowledge of wine that gave me the ability to be able to sell exactly what I thought my customer would be satisfied and happy with. Being able to answer questions related to your product but also being able to *ask* questions to **understand** your customer's taste is a big advantage. I can get clues about someone's taste in wine just by knowing how he prefers to drink his coffee for example (no sugar, medium sweet, etc).

It's a pity, making a very good approach, making a good impression and instantly ruin it by making a wrong decision about the product you sold because of the lack of specialization. If you're working in a fish restaurant,for example, try to educate yourself about fish, learn which ones have more bones than others, which ones are more delicate and which ones have more fat in their meat, also learn how to debone each fish and taste as many as possible to gain the specialization and be able to identify your customer's taste.

No matter your field of action, try to learn as many things as possible about the product you are trying to sell. This is what will separate you from others and how you will improve your selling skills. When you are able to identify your customer's taste you have another clue for your mind's script which will lead you closer to maximum value!

Body Language

We are moving more and more to the practical part of a sale. Body language is a very important factor because it reveals most aspects of yourself that we were analyzing in the first part of the book! To be more precise, your body language will reveal:

1) Your level of confidence

2) Your energy

If you haven't done the self-improvement that we talked about before and your confidence is low, your body language will reveal it 90% of the time. Maybe not instantly if things go exactly how you planned them to, but as soon as you find the first obstacle in your sale, for instance, a question about your product that you don't know the answer to, you will make an expression, a hand gesture, maybe your voice will start trembling a bit which reveals that you are not so confident as you seemed to be. On the other hand, if you have done the self-improvement and you don't fake your confidence but it's naturally high, you don't even have to think of such things that may happen. Because some things could be done by mistake or lack of experience even if your confidence is high, we will go through some things you need to avoid and others that you should aim for!

Avoid touching a client, especially if you don't know him very well because instead of building a friendly vibe it's very repulsive. Think of yourself talking to a receptionist in the hotel you just went to check-in. He shows you around and as you reach your room he touches you lightly on your back and says ''have a nice stay''. It would be very awkward at least!

Avoid intense facial expressions and also **use hand gestures very carefully**. A hand gesture can reveal a calm state but it can show nervousness as well, try to move your hands smooth enough to seem sharp but not nervous as well. When approaching your customer keep a distance of at least ½ meter and don't ''invade'' his/her personal space.

From another perspective, you are not the only one being observed. You are also an **observer** of your client's body language. You can use the hints you find to **adjust your behavior**. If you see him being nervous you should try to talk a bit slower and make him feel more relaxed. If you see him a bit hesitant you can try to smile a bit more instead of being very serious. If you see him a bit tipsy you can catch the vibe and maybe say something funny to build a good connection. Be a good *observer*, you have the advantage if you observe and adjust accordingly!

The next thing your body language reveals as we mentioned is your *energy*. The first thing I want to highlight is this: *It's very important to give someone the energy that says "I have something interesting to tell you" instead of "I want to sell you something"*. In the first case you make someone curious about what it is that you have to propose and in the second one subconsciously, you put him in a defensive state where he has to protect his money from the aggressive person who wants to sell him something. A smile always helps with this.

Also, be aware of the *tone of your voice*. You can use it to create the specific feeling that you want to transfer to someone. For example, a louder tone of voice could mean certainty and a lower one could mean that you understand someone and his situation. Use it as your weapon to adjust to each different situation and build a connection of trust!

Another very important thing you want to keep in balance is your *level of excitement.* A certain level of excitement is very helpful to build a good atmosphere and reach maximum value but what I figured out is that it's very easy to overdo it and seem like you want to close this sale so badly. You want to adjust your level of excitement and even when you see that your sale is going even better than you thought, try to stay calm, keep the same voice level, keep the same body language and don't start moving quicker or speak quicker for example because it shows that you're over-excited and makes your customer think that something must be wrong here when actually everything is fine!

Implied Value and association with Poker

In the game of Poker there is a term called **implied value**. It refers to the situation where you don't have a made hand yet, but instead a draw to a very good hand and you face a bet. In this case implied value refers to the justification of your decision to call the bet with the chance of hitting your draw and make a very strong hand, thus your potential winnings can be very high.

The way this relates to sales is simple. You don't always have to aim for the most expensive thing to get maximum value from someone. Sometimes you have to trust your judgment and think of the **potential benefits** IF your customer finally likes the initial product. These benefits can be winning a customer and making him a regular, getting a second product (e.g. another bottle of the same wine) right after the first one, increase the bond of trust between the customer and you. All these can be taken into account and not always consider that you made a bad sell when you don't sell the most expensive thing possible.

I will give an example of the power of excitement but also implied value on a sale when you keep it under the right balance. Last year I was in a major wine tasting in London where I found some Greek producers who recently got into the British wine market. I have tasted their wines several times in Greece and I thought It would be an excellent addition to our wine list. The problem is, my manager was quite hesitant since Greek wine is not so famous outside Greece and he was not sure if it was going to be profitable. The next day I ordered 4 different wines of 4 bottles each from the same producer. The manager said that it's all on me and I had to take accountability if they stay on the shelf for a long time or so. You see, I was so positive because I knew the value of the product, having the knowledge to evaluate wines, and also I was super excited to make a debut for Greek wine in the restaurant. The wines arrived after a couple of days and on the same day of the arrival, we had a reservation for a group of 14 doctors. Following the evaluation process, I knew that I can push for what I wanted considering the high financial level. The guests arrived, They chose a menu of 8 courses and they wanted to have a look at the wine list. I handed over the list saying just this little thing ''Please take your time and have a look. If you're looking for something different for tonight we have some new arrivals of Greek wine which are not yet on the wine list and could be a perfect pairing for your courses''. That's the only thing I said and didn't push

35

any further. You see, metaphorically, this is like putting a small bait in the hook so you can catch a big fish. The gentleman who was looking at the list finally decided to go for a Bordeaux Cru Bourgeois, a very nice red wine from France, and another french Viognier (white wine). I served the wines, but after a couple of minutes, it seems that many people at the table were not so satisfied with the decision and the wines seemed a bit out of their tasting preferences. So the gentleman I was talking to before asked for the wine list again and as I handed it over to him he asked me: ''What about the Greek wines that you mentioned before?'' This question was all I wanted to hear because that night, I sold ALL 16 bottles of Greek wine to these people. I didn't have to talk too much or push anyone to buy, I just knew that I had a very good product of high value and what I just did is plant a little idea on their head, make it seem that there is no need for them to buy it because they will be sold anyway and instead there is a good chance that they are losing on something of great value here. In addition, it didn't matter that the Greek wines were a bit cheaper than the first bottles they chose because the implied value was that they bought all of them and this justified my decision. Nobody understood how this was possible the moment we have a wine list of 200+ different wines and we sold out all 16 bottles of wine that were not even on the list! Abundance mindset, knowledge, and the right approach is everything you need!

12 of the 16 bottles totally sold that night
Artichoke Restaurant, London (1 Michelin Star)

A numbers game: Selling in an abundant environment

It's not the easiest thing to stay positive, calm, and not get too excited when making a sale in a very limited environment. When you're working in a place where it's not so busy, there are not many people coming in and very few choices for you to sell something, it's really hard to seem relaxed and have the confidence that you would have in a very busy environment. Maybe, if that's the case, you have to consider finding a job that will provide the standards for you to play the **numbers game**.

Since you are, hypothetically saying, improved in all aspects that we mentioned before what comes next is that you play the numbers game in an abundant environment. When you got let's say 100 people approximately that you will have the chance to sell something in one day, it doesn't affect you that much If you couldn't close one sale, because you're moving straight to the next one. Otherwise, if there are 10 people that you will have the chance to talk to all day, It will certainly affect you in some way psychologically, because you just lost 1/10 of the chances to sell something that day. Even before you close the sale, your energy is going to seem like you're trying to sell to the last person on this planet, thus being in a scarcity mindset.

From another perspective, it's also very helpful to have many choices on the products you want to sell. Let's say you're trying to sell cocktails. The place you work has only 5 cocktails on its list. These are not ideal conditions for your mission, even if you are experienced with sales! You may do good but you would be better in a place with, let's say 50 different cocktails, where you can find the best product for each person based on your specialization, knowledge, and preferences he/she has.

Try to find a job that meets your needs and gives you the chance to shine and reach your full potential. If you are already in the right environment, you should focus on your mindset and techniques and start playing the numbers game!

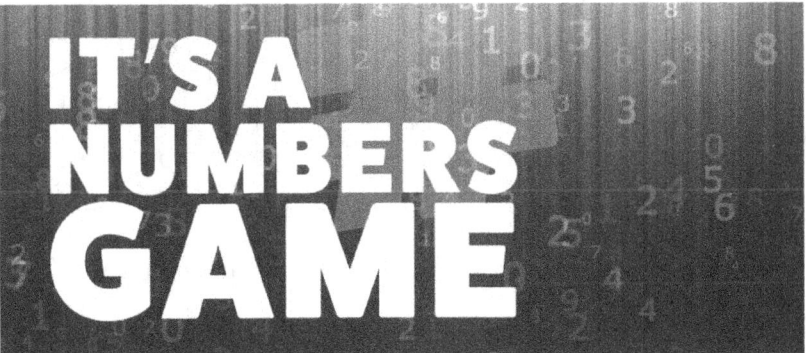

Further thoughts on sales

Improvement on sales has further benefits for life in general. You would be surprised if you notice how many things in life are very similar to sales. Some examples include success on dating, succeeding on job interviews, becoming a better observer on situations, and all in all **improving every aspect and situation which is confidence related**. The key in everything that you try to master is to **break it down** into smaller simpler parts and work on them **individually**. It may seem a bit out of the ordinary or sometimes a bit funny for someone to see the thinking process and all the factors that are taken into account for someone to become successful on a specific thing. This is why only a few people become very **successful** at what they do and most people stay on an average level. Because some people prefer to laugh while others work on their purpose and eventually succeed. If sales is a big part of your job and you still wonder if it's worth putting in the effort to succeed, I can assure you that you will be satisfied in the long run!

Epilogue

As I promised, this book does not consist of endless pages with every possible strategy for every possible scenario. The goal of this book is to make the reader a master-key that can adapt on every lock and not search for 100 different keys to open 100 different doors. I believe that once you understand the fundamentals, the details become the easy part. I'm also positive that if you reached this part of the book you gained extra motivation to grow and improve as well as another perspective on sales which I believe and hope will be extremely beneficial. The format of the book being single-read offers the advantage for someone to go through multiple reads and eventually understand the critical parts in a relatively short amount of time.

I hope that I could help, lit a spark on someone's mind to become very successful in sales. At this point, I'd like to think of what I said in the first pages and if the younger version of me would be glad to read this book. I think he definitely would...

Konstantinos Chatzimitakos

''The Shard'' London

02/03/2020

www.ingramcontent.com/pod-product-compliance
Lightning Source LLC
Chambersburg PA
CBHW071120220526
45467CB00004B/1969